No F*cks Left to Give!

A Survival Guide for Times Like These

by Lou Bortone, Author of "F*ck You, Pay Me!"

ISBN-13: 978-0-9994596-2-1

© Lou Bortone. All Rights Reserved.

This page intentionally left blue.

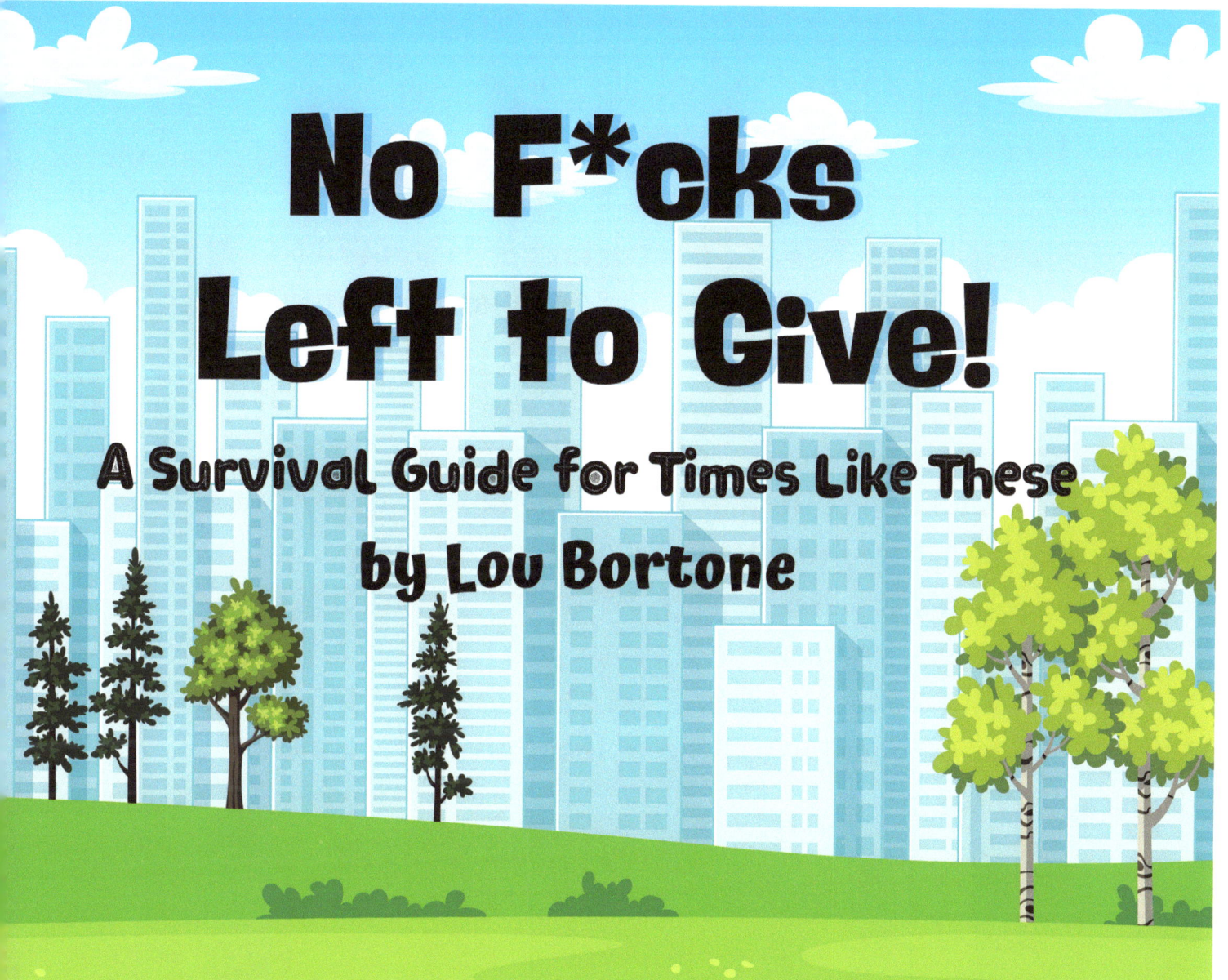

No F*cks Left to Give!

A Survival Guide for Times Like These

by Lou Bortone

ISBN: 978-0-9994596-2-1

© Lou Bortone. All Rights Reserved.

Dedication

This silly book on a serious subject is dedicated to the thousands of medical professionals, health care providers, first responders, service workers, public servants, and men and women on the front lines of battling this global pandemic. Whether you're stocking shelves at grocery stores or caring for the sick, we appreciate your courage and sacrifice. Some folks don't have the luxury of "social distancing" or "sheltering in place." We thank you for your service. And for anyone else who might be down to their last f*ck, here's hoping we can at least give a f*ck about each other!

Lou Bortone

There once was a gal who was fresh out of fucks,
Her name was Lucinda, but her friends called her Luxe.
She was fed up and had no fucks left to give,
There may be no more for as long as she'd live.

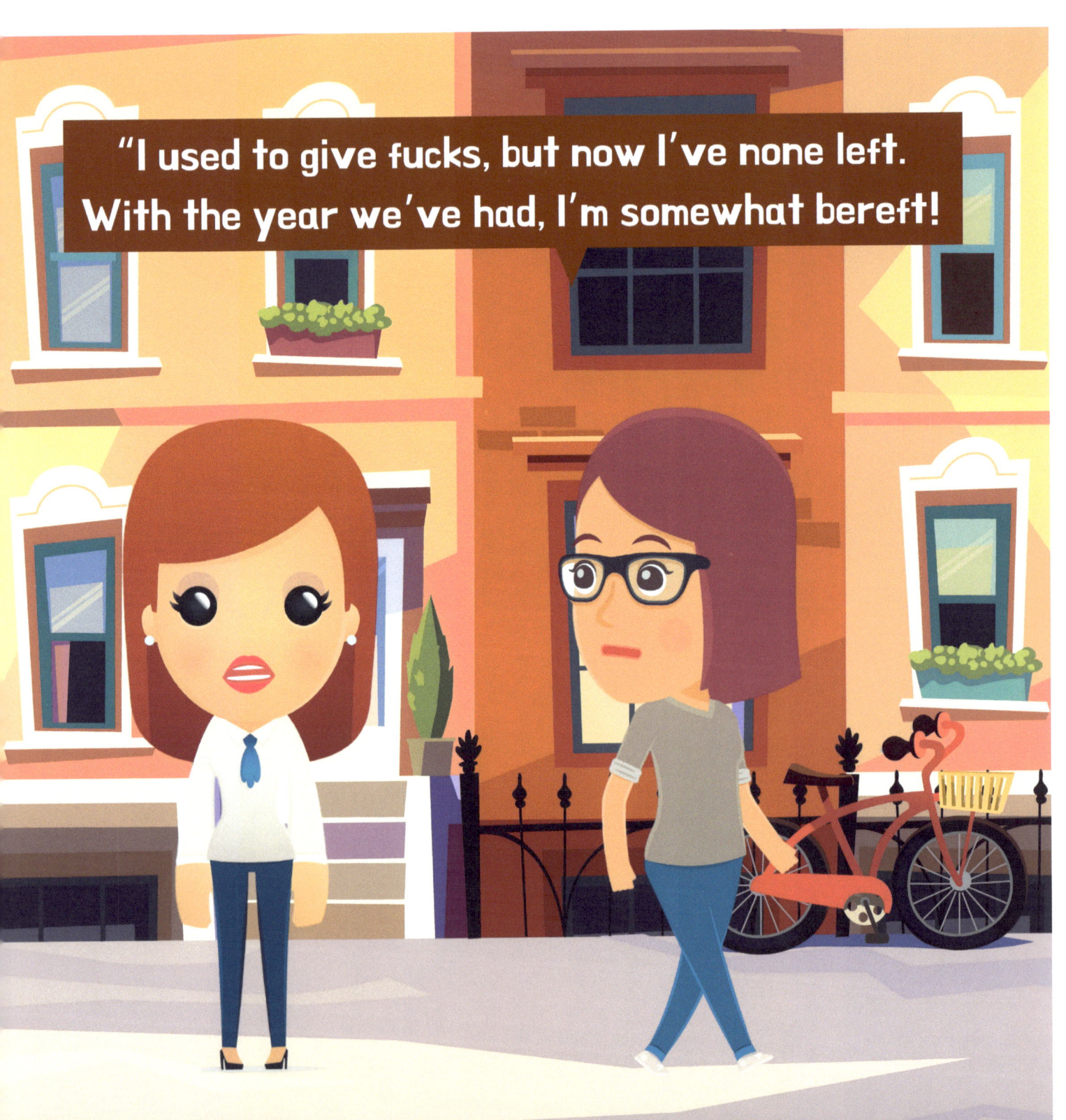

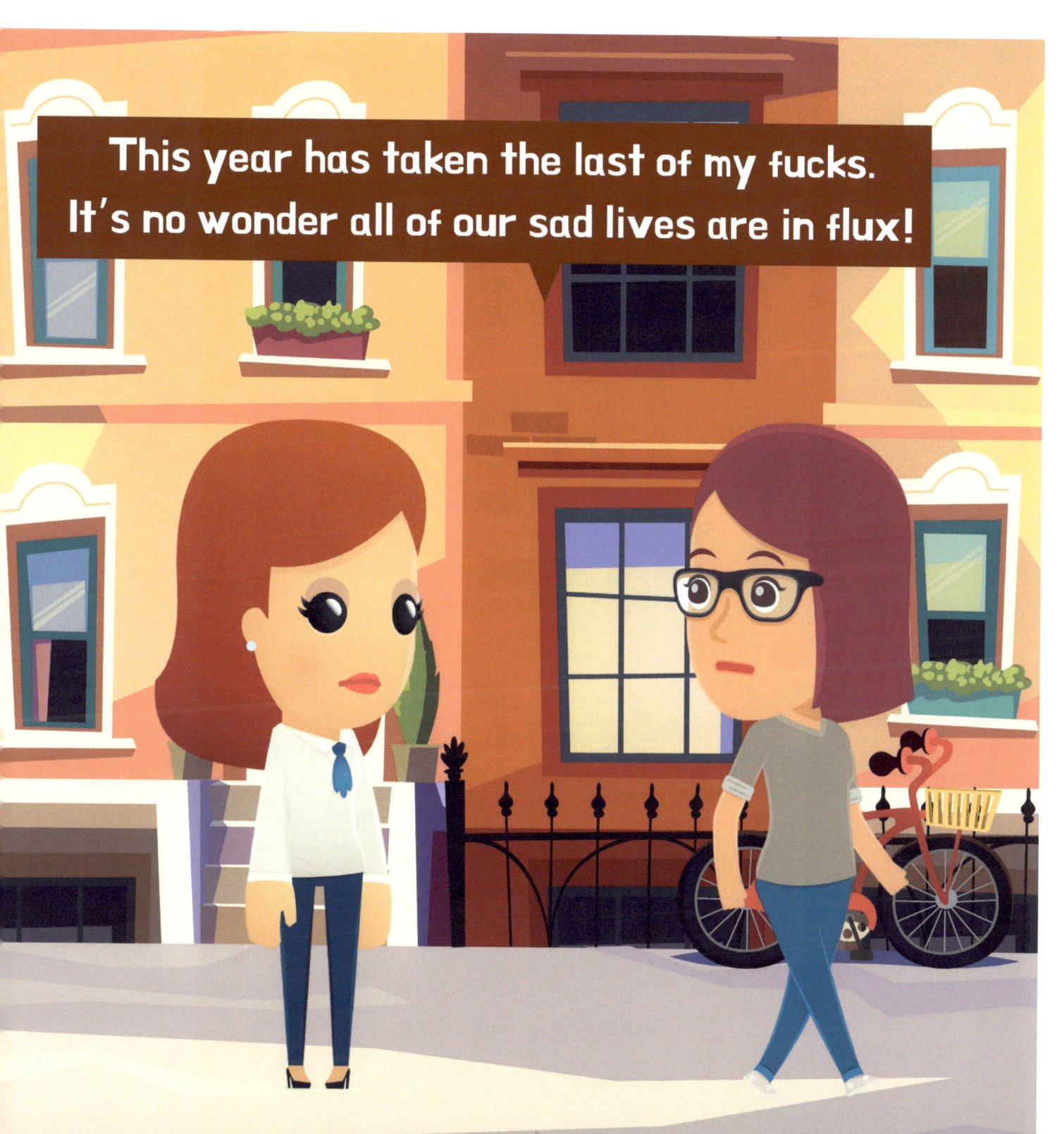

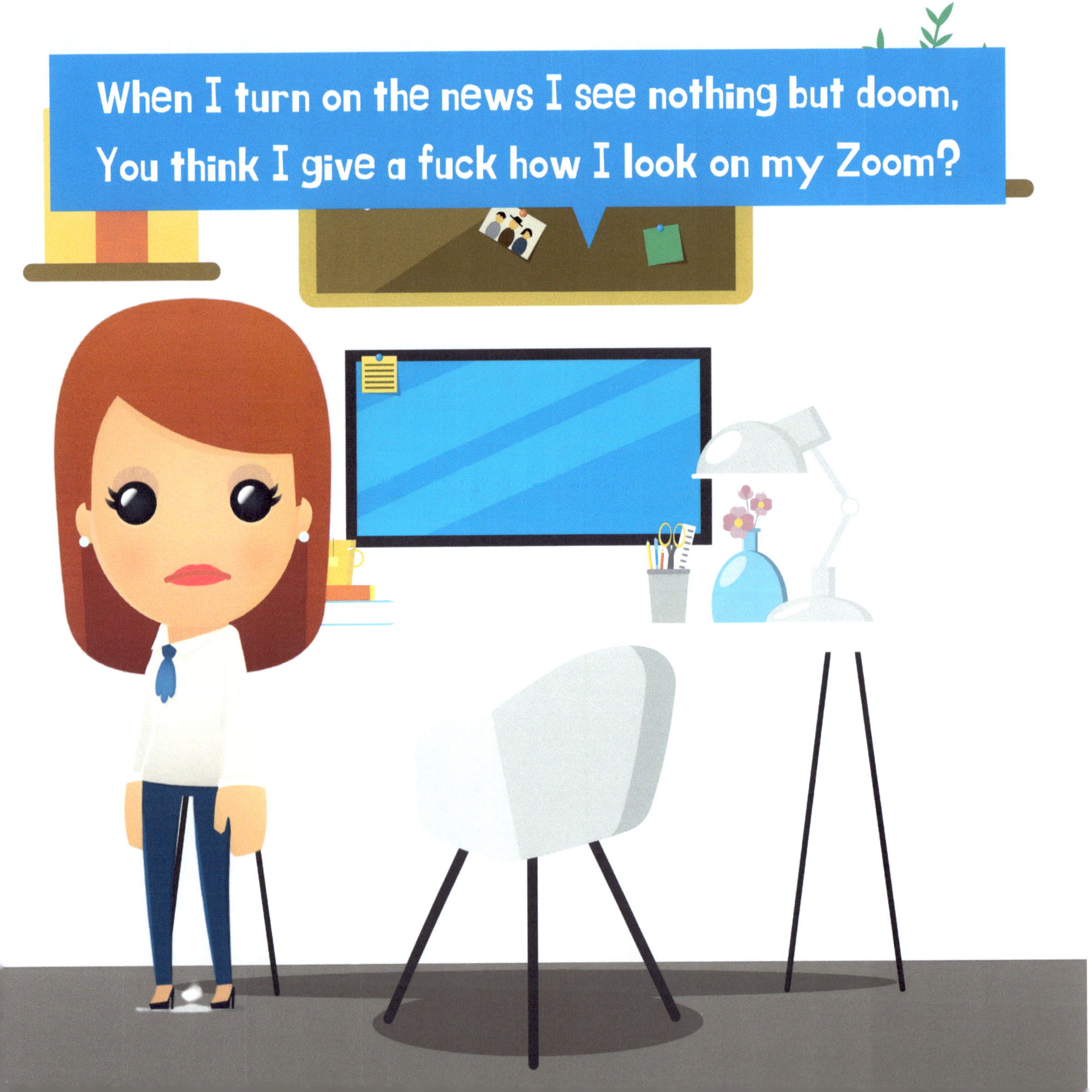

I don't care what frigging Netflix series I'm binging,
Got my ass on the couch and I'm sitting here cringing.

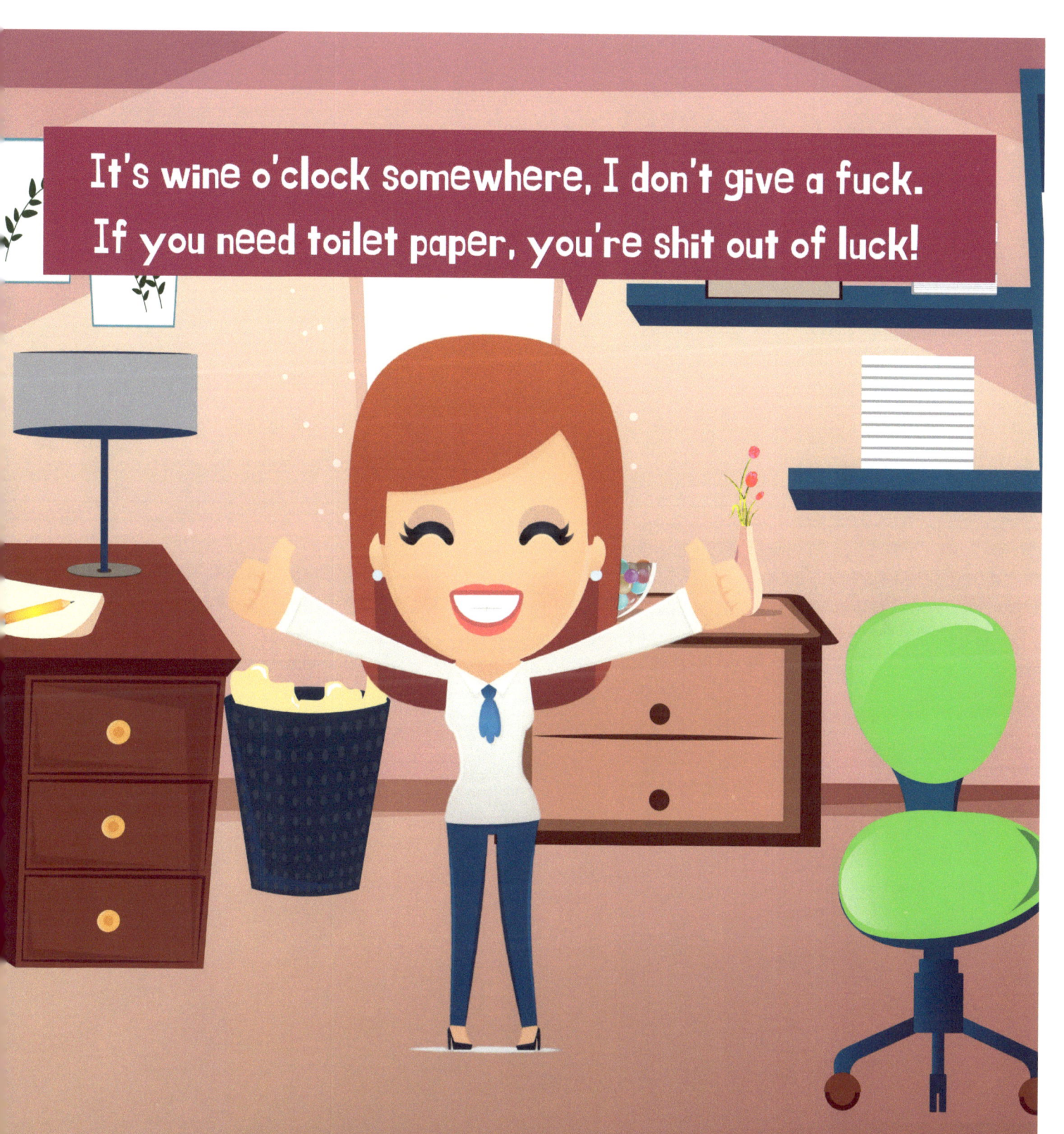

So that's that, my friend, I've got no fucks left to give!
Covid has left my poor brain like a sieve!

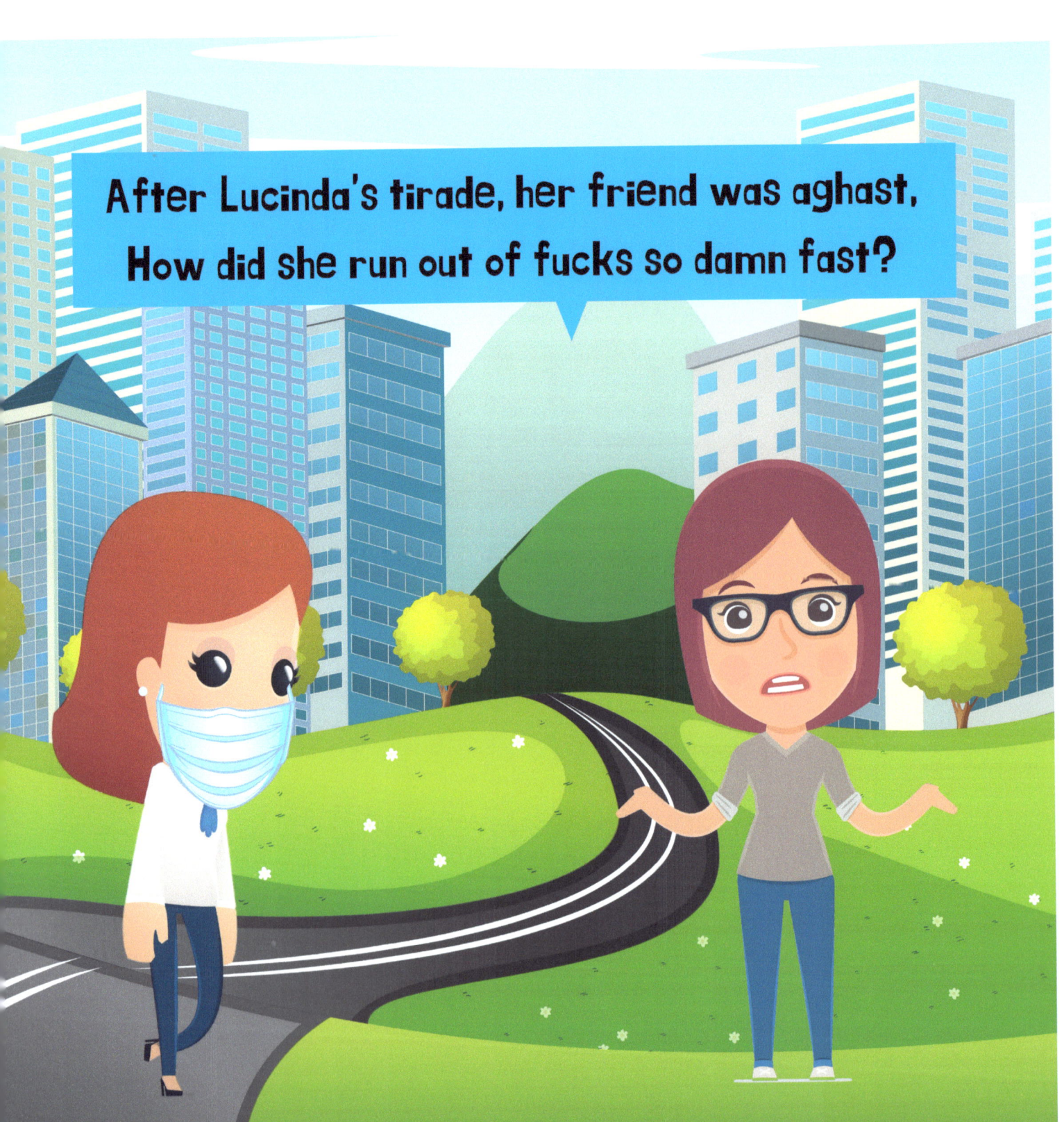

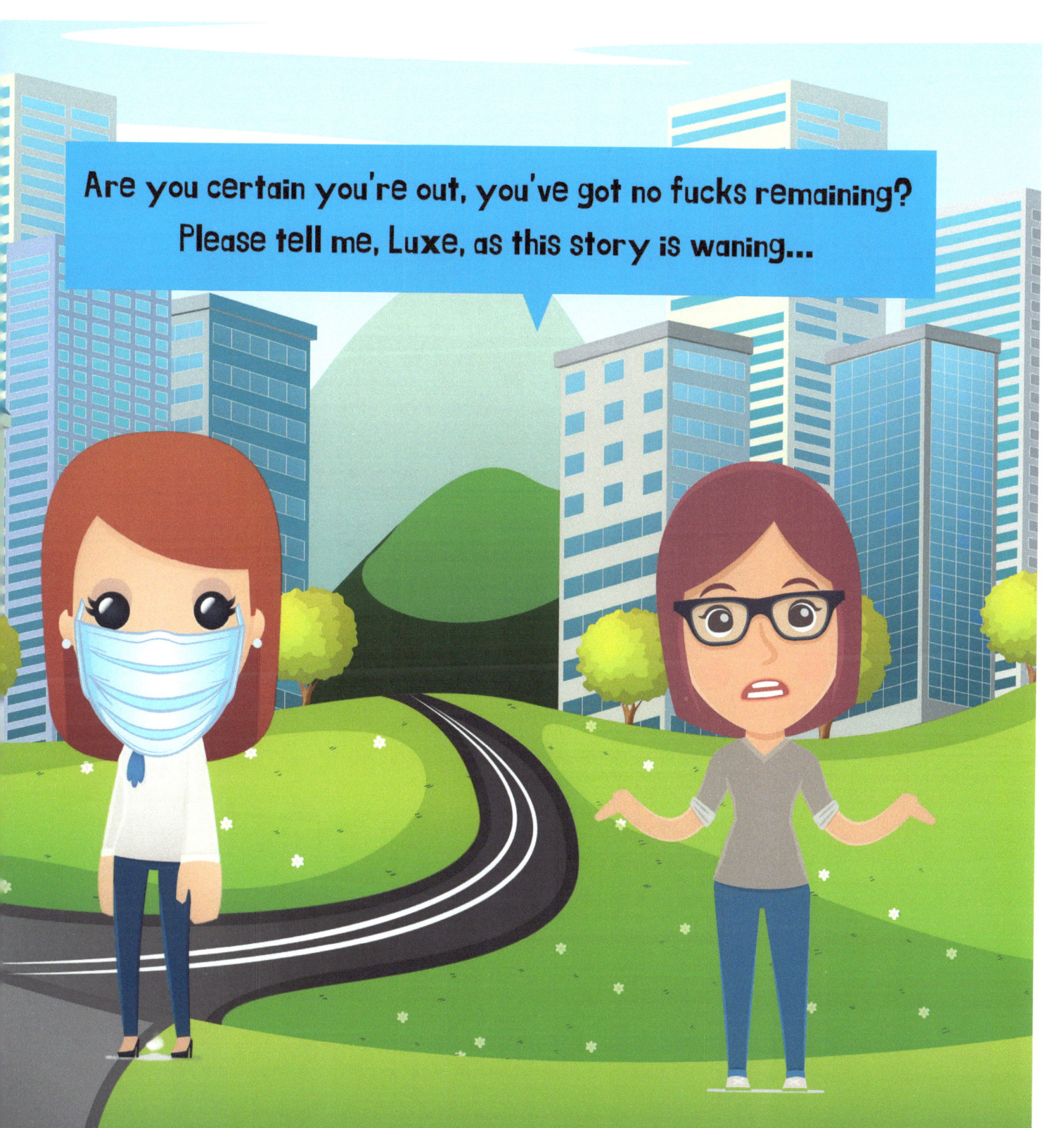

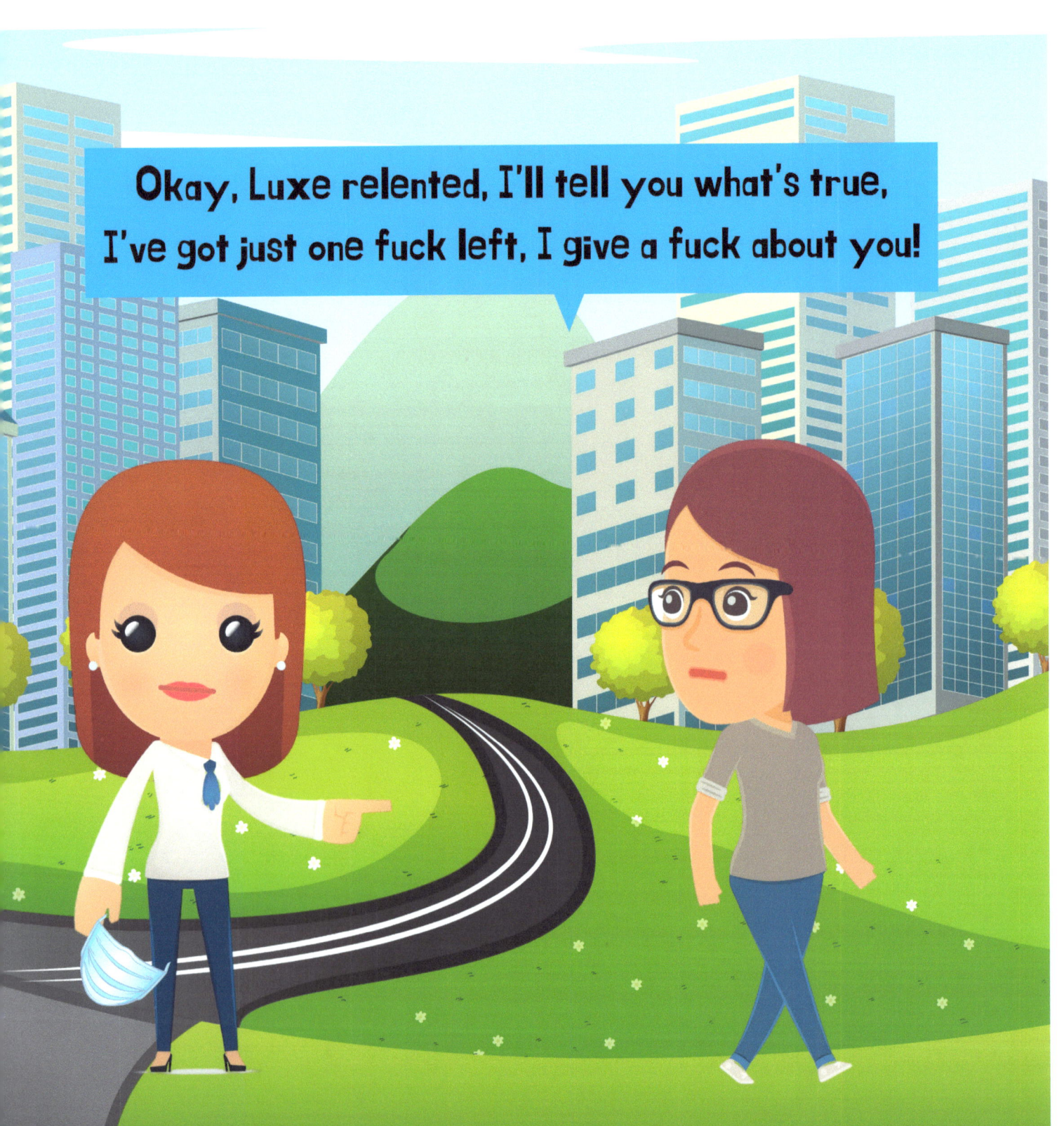

But don't tell anyone for as long as you live,
'Coz it's more fun to have zero fucks left to give!

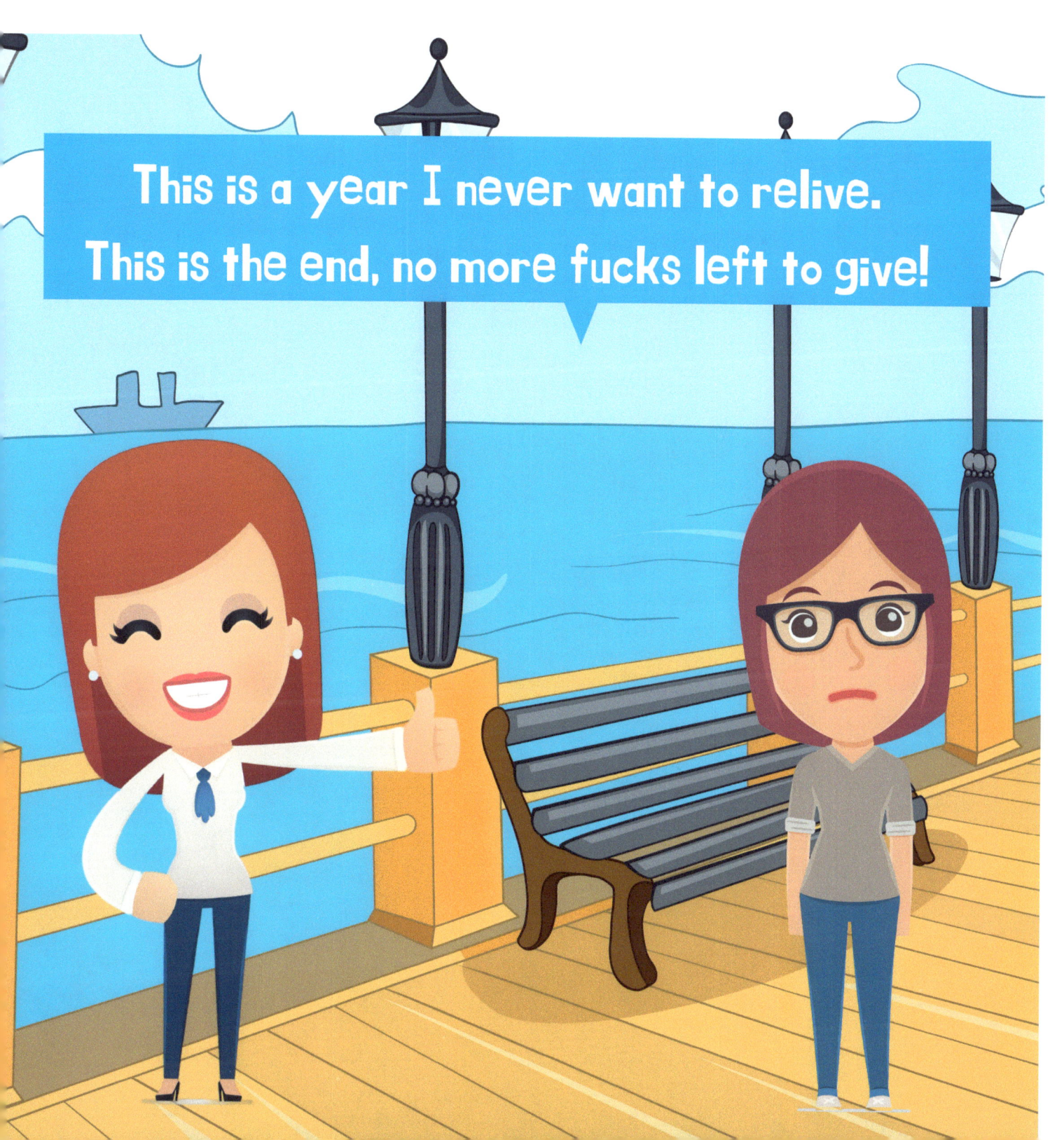

Lou Bortone

Lou Bortone is known as The Video Godfather. We're not exactly sure why and, frankly, we're a little afraid to ask. What we do know is that Lou Bortone has been a pioneer and thought leader in the video space since the launch of YouTube in 2005. He's helped thousands of entrepreneurs and companies create and leverage online video to build their brands and dramatically grow their revenues.

Prior to his industry leading work in online video marketing, Lou spent over 20 years as a marketing executive in the television and entertainment industries, including stints as National Promotion Manager for E! Entertainment Television and Senior Vice President of Marketing for Fox Family Worldwide in Los Angeles.

Lou is a popular speaker, author, and ghostwriter of six business books. He's also the author of "Video Marketing Rules: How to Win in a World Gone Video." You can learn more about Lou at LouBortone.com.

www.LouBortone.com

Get your own "done for you" illustrated book at: www.FunFabBook.com

Do you have a story to tell or a message to share? An illustrated and/or irreverent book is the perfect way to bring attention and awareness to you and your message. I write and create books like this for clients! They are completely "done-for-you" and can even include a website to sell your book, as well as setting up your book on Amazon. Intrigued? Email me at vip@loubortone.com or visit www.FunFabBook.com for details!

Also by Lou Bortone:

"F*ck You PayMe!"
"Stay The F*ck Home"
"Dump The Duds"
"Quit Bitching, Start Pitching"

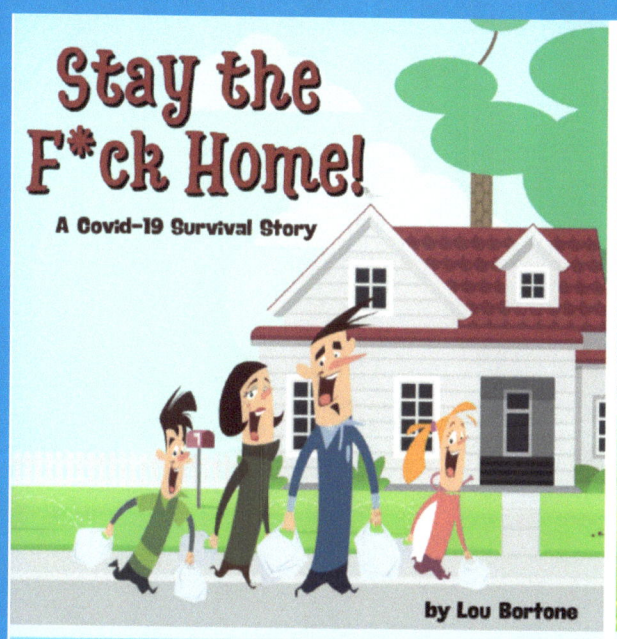
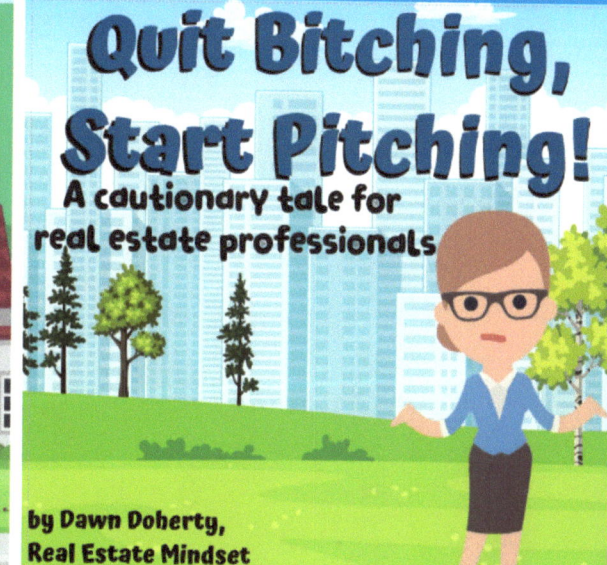

Get your own "done for you" illustrated book at:
www.FunFabBook.com